W9-AHC-668

For my dozens and dozens of wonderful cousins.
— S.F.

ISBN 0-439-70066-3

Book design by Elizabeth B. Parisi
Photography by Nimkin/Parrinello and Saxton Freymann

12 11 10 9 8 7 6 5 4 3 2 1   4 5 6 7 8 9/0

Printed in Mexico   49

First printing, July 2004

Baby Food

SCHOLASTIC INC.
New York Toronto London Auckland Sydney
Mexico City New Delhi Hong Kong Buenos Aires

Puppy

Kitten

Bunny

Baby hippo

Chick

Baby mouse

Duckling

Penguin chick

Piglet

Owlet

Kangaroo
joey

Seal pup

Armadillo pup

Lion cub

Bear cub

Baby monkey

Baby giraffe

Whale calf

Elephant calf

Baby octopus

Tadpole

**Turtle
hatchling**

Spiderling

Caterpillar

And me!